Gallery Books
Editor Peter Fallon
THE THING IS

Peter Sirr

THE THING IS

Gallery Books

The Thing Is
is first published
simultaneously in paperback
and in a clothbound edition
on 24 September 2009.

The Gallery Press
Loughcrew
Oldcastle
County Meath
Ireland

www.gallerypress.com

ISBN 978 1 85235 473 2 *paperback*
        978 1 85235 474 9 *clothbound*

A CIP catalogue record for this book
is available from the British Library.

Contents

for Enda and Freya

An Opening

For everything, for nothing
chestnuts on the lane
leaves at the door

for the thinning trees
for ditches
for watery fields

for the firewood, the fire
for the hob, the kettle
for the cold

for the rain and its skies
for the fox, the vixen
for the porch light

the postman's van
for the furious winds
chimney music

for ash, for hazel
for heron, for swan
for standing in the lane

no one, nowhere
and so lightened
nothing's left

everything begun.

Music for Viols

Tobias Hume's 'Good Againe'

Good again
this night, this late,
to hear that tune and fall
again, the slow dark drag,
texture
of thickly branched trees
swaying above water,
of sound moving
from the farthest pit
to pour down.
God and the devil
must play the viol.
The door of the world
swings open
on Hume's excited figure.
After sadness, hunger,
royal blindness
to the great shame of this land
and those that do not help me
after a bellyful of snails
and the sniping of lutenists,
good again to stand
with the night
in Jordi's hands
and listen
and walk in
as far as the tune will go.

Thanksgiving Hymn

after Brecht

Praise the night and the darkness round you.
Come in droves
and look up at the sky.
Already the day has passed you by.

Praise your neighbours, the grass and animals,
observe how like you
they must live
and just like you must die.

Praise the tree, built on corpses, soaring to heaven;
praise the corpses;
praise the tree they nourish
and also praise heaven.

From the bottom of your heart praise heaven's
terrible memory; it has long forgotten
your name, your face.
No one knows you exist.

Praise the cold, the darkness, the decay.
Have a good look;
nothing depends on you;
relax, you can die with an easy conscience.

Ode to Beginning

after Brecht

Pure
joy of beginning, dawnlight
on the kitchen flags, first grass,
when green has been forgotten,
first page of the new book
waiting on the table:

read it slowly, as long as you can
hold on to surprise, hymn
first things, first splash
of water on your face, first touch
of shirt on skin,

the beginning of love, that
first shy
avoiding glance . . .
the beginning of work,
first touch of the wheel
and the engine sparking life,

first coffee, first cigarette
hitting the spot, first thought . . .

Shhh

SHHH .

The counter intelligence community registers its disquiet
too many of us now, too much getting out

it's an awkward day for dentists as the case drags on
and no one much is smiling now, not the firemen

nor the baggage handlers, nurses, first time buyers
and since they changed the city boundaries and lowered the fares

my taxi driver's blue with rage, who never asked anyone to live
in Celbridge
or fucking Maynooth, but what it must be to sit back in the
evening

with your tooth repaired and your bags intact, watching
the last of the light revive the carpet and know

you've passed your five-yearly vetting review, your grandparents
haven't let you down, your teenage son, your childhood friend

haven't spilled the beans, no one has marched from the grave
to rattle his bones and bloody the carpet, and you are whole
again

a re-trusted member of the counter intelligence community
your swipe card unlocks the canteen again, knowledge swamps
the room

and you can cross the boundaries with your ear to the ground
your eyes on the cockpit, your whole body

as long as it lasts pressed to the pulse of the unquiet planet. *Shhh!*

ELECTRICITY SPEAKS

Electricity speaks your language, no translation necessary
everybody is afraid of electricity, and rightfully so

Nova Products says: it's possible to use anything for torture
but it's a little easier to use our devices

and someone sits quietly in an office high above the traffic
filling in the requisition order: three black, four white, three
    pearl

software tracks the invoices, the multilingual client feedback
    forms
proofread at an excellent rate and posted on the site.

THE NEW REGIME INHERITS THE ELECTRODES

Software lives and is replicated, it's a code re-use
the new regime inherits the electrodes

and it's a long day with a busy agenda
tunable munitions, psychotronics, voice to skull technologies

coffee in a foam cup and networking in the information hall
Electronic Intelligence offers The House of Fun torture
    chamber

here on the border the algorithms multiply, where peace
is not always human and not always lethal

self-deciding sentinels clean out the zone
denying access, keeping costs down.

OLD

Software registers the schoolgirl
taken to the Railway Square at dawn
where the judge stands impatient, the noose in his hands

today's small story
heaped outside the morgue
green cords around the necks, the bodies drilled with holes

old enough to die
in a hail of bombs in the ancient city,
who clamber up the bulletins now

and fall back
to the quenched playgrounds
and the silence of the search engines.

FOR THE HANGED BOYS

For the hanged boys
what? An eternity unviolated

that they walk together
through the alleys of paradise

that they lie down
in the name of nothing but themselves

that they lie unwatched, untouched
their bodies restored

as the unreachable cities
fade and fall, the squares

silent and the cranes
disassembled, the applauding hands

disassembled, gone to bone, dust,
in the name of nothing scattered to the winds.

A DREAM

Software conceals the electrodes, relentless
engines trawl the planet but the truth
is post-processed and harmless. Here
the vanished maps, the stalled tanks and the dead
returned, here the eternally inviolate
harvest and harvesters, the voices soft in the dusk.

The Different Rains Come Down

For motto the darting snipe,
the curlew, the tree house
to which every morning I climb
bearing with aplomb
a flask of coffee, last night's line.

*

Deep in the hut the silence
roots. Days here. How long?
The meadow sings all day.
Reed-song, the lake spreads its music.

*

Yesterday
travelling though the country again
in the old jalopy, down the little roads
with only the graveyards signed
the dead handing us on
from townland to townland
until we found the junction.

*

I lift the binoculars, scanning a field
the sun has fallen on, has
fallen for, and soaked with light

in the middle a tree
like everyone's memory.

*

Mist this morning
the hedges webbed with dew.

*

September breakfast:
a mouthful of blackberries in the lane.

*

I lift the binoculars: intimacies
of trees and cattle

sudden drift of smoke
sudden flitting on a wire
sudden roof
bats, suddenly,
like too fast films

suddenscape.

*

Crex crex
in the callows
the corncrake survives
to be counted by the Corncrake Officer —
is it not all
I could ever have wanted?

*

The lake lies half hidden
at the end of the meadow, sending out
its reed legions

to sway drunkenly as they struggle
with the burden of the water.

*

On the days he's not there
I tramp to my friend's house on the hill
and make coffee in his kitchen, I drink
from his mug, look out from his window
down towards the grey splash of the lake.
Still there, my mute swans, my life!
My friend sweats in the city
or has crept into my hut to drink from my mug
and train my binoculars on the gap between the trees
into his own distant life.

*

The different rains come down
differently orchestrated
configurations of the rain
on corrugated iron
winter music, summer song
small surprise
of the secondary rain of trees
an after rain
bestowed like a gift
as you enter the canopy.

*

Whatever you were
you scared the dog
and made him whimper

welcome or warning
your eyes shone
at the edge of the light

and the signs were all there
that absolute dark
the sound you made

as you ran down the road
almost colliding with us
before slipping into the field

or you were nothing
neither curse nor blessing
you were

yourself purely, your eyes blazing
caught in the porch glow
where you circled behind us

to take us in. Cold-eyed
briefly curious
and quickly gone

you left behind
a living dark, the black road
suddenly crowded

and the night filling like a corridor
all of us are passing through
with hardly a breath

between us . . .

*

Standing outside in the evening quiet
avid for light, for how the trees collect it,
disburse it, how the lower branches shine
with a colour combed out of the lake
and washed with reeds

listening to the sound a place makes
flittings and undersongs stitched into the air,
the creaturely silence, things
shifting and loosening,
a wren now from the eaves

darting to grass, then hesitating back;
standing at the edge of it as if to inhabit
some part of the conversation,
but just the way a hesitation inhabits a language,
no wren codes, deciphered trees

but standing there like nothing at all,
a post brushed by moth-wings,
a stillness rent with little cries,
a body thinned to bone like a hook
the mind might throw its hat on and forget.

The Overgrown Path

A CORNER

Nothing, hardly anything, just
these few steps from the door of the restaurant
down half the length of Chatham Street, as far as the corner
where I look over and see, suddenly, how close you are,
what *gravid* means, how we are walking slowly out of our old
    lives
and nothing flutters or halts us or puts out flags

and I want to stop, hold on, loiter
not much, not forever, nor awash with it but just
a little longer, I want to walk these yards
enjoying the sun, the throng, our slow progress,
I want to reach back to the restaurant
for a glass to toast you with, a history

of lunch specials, of Saturdays, for pillars of salt
to dissolve as we keep on looking in every direction
and some delicate canister to shake
the grains of this minute on the rest of the journey
as we promise to gather what we can of the future
and shake it back, over our shoulders, on this corner.

WAITING

We say your name and wait.
We wait and say your name.
We see you everywhere:
on the street,
behind the counter,
throwing bread on water, watching
the fold-up swans.
The swans have your past, your future.
There's not an inch
of this long canal
you don't know at least as well
as the lost navigators.
Sometimes I wake up
in a confusion of joy, an
access of it, as if I too had been
as intently waited for
and certain we'd always moved
towards this, all of us
cajoled into light,
our flat-out souls
or the ghosts
of everlasting waiting
up there, pacing their corridors
fraught, expectant, wanting
to give it all to us again.

PPS

Welcome 3755547K
your small head rests
in the arms of the state
your fingers are counted, your toes
registered, your cries
have found their way
to a vault of need, you're
known, allowed for, admitted
though mysterious to us
and as yet unpersuaded
you drift and sway
and kick against the world
but listen
your breath moves in a far drawer
a number among numbers
you shift in your folder
you open your eyes
you fall through the letterbox
and climb the stairs
you float towards your basket
and gently surrender
ah 3755547K
recognized, acknowledged, filed,
let the complex systems
convince, sleep
on the miracle of your name
spilling across the screen,
the long arms of the sun reaching in.

LUNAR

Dear pea-head, in your lunar language
tell us again how the world stirs,
how things appear, hold still, drift;
how the light startles and the dog erupts
at dawn to shout creation down,
how smiles begin and faces blunder close
then far, and sing. Give us the seal-note,
bird-trill, warble, let rip, tell us
what the gods want of us, who your leader is,
how to sing, like you, under the language,
like stars, like submarines, like the spirits
of everything here, like a sleeve of wrens
loosed from a hedgerow and lifted clear . . .

CLOONCUNNY

Nothing happens here that I know about.
The land lies quiet, the ash trees are silent,
the dog slumbers on the window ledge, the swans
have disappeared into the rushes again.
If it weren't for the gas cylinders, the rusting tap,
the improvised line and yesterday's papers on the table
how would we know we were here?
The teapot dozes, the kitchen roll is palaeolithic,

the weeds poke through the stones. Nothing happens here
that I know about. My wife sleeps in the other room,
my daughter is pinned to her cross of sleep,
the lilies shine from their pads, the rushes
move like water, the ash trees have woken
and are glittering in the breeze, wrens leap
from the hedges and sing elaborately, a heron
commands the airspace, swoops down, becomes a branch.

TONGUES

The sun dipped its beams through the clouds and sank
on a bed of cinders above the lake, not that I could tell you this
or point it out, though I needed the sky, the warblers
starting up, the bats blundering out, the mown grass
the smell of all that day: hay and spilled petrol and baby shit
and rancour, the stink of argument, spew of insults
and now wanting to say, let these argue for us, make our case
evidence of the cindery sky, bank of purpling cloud
the darkening fields and trees, that gaggle of ash
on the brow of the hill above the lake, and later, in the worst of it
the rake shining in the moonlight, the slash-hook,
the long handled shears, the potted plants, the black lake,
any of them, all of them, if only
we can hold our tongues, if only we can find them.

ANTARCTICAS

Don't we see
Antarctica in your eyes, and hear
the landmasses quake in your laughter,

and doesn't the whole world shift when you go out
in your Peruvian hat? We're watching you,
we're busy with our endless preparations,

but already you fall between the cracks,
you slip through our fingers, you have
somehow worked free of the straps and harnesses

and move, delightedly, towards the dangerous places.

CONCERT GOING

Welcome to the language
I'm trying to say, this morpheme is me
and this is you
this is the sound of food arriving
at the castle gate
this is the drawbridge
stalled and unmoving
these the morose inhabitants
silent and unyielding
these units are hitting the floor
this is the dog indignant again
hello black cat dark yard sudden
semantic flurry, the neighbour annoyed
and rain falling down like rice on the floor
this is your mouth
where the food goes
like Shakespeare to his theatre
all the tumblers ever
to have fallen down for fun
and up and down again
like rain and dark cats
and long centuries
of the indignation of dogs
and then you smile
and wave the sounds around
then looping, coiling, prancing
come the madrigalists, bell shakers, robed
choristers riffing, the dense
delighted hedgerows
of your voices
and everything else can wait
all the signs can snooze
the sun spill in the yard

more than we remember of it
and language sit an aeon yet
its small waters muttering
in a corner of the field . . .

POEM

I'm writing this under your nose
under everything you're saying
under the news at one
under the roadkills and marriage breakups
I'm writing it in the eyes
of the woman in the laundrette this afternoon
there it is, inscribing itself
in the bottom of the milk glass
and there again
Untitled1, unsaved, fallen
through a crack in the system, reconstructed
on the counter between classes
it collects for the Capuchins it eats St Anthony's bread
it follows the exhausted horses to the enclosure
it stays too long at the junction
it follows us up the stairs to bed
it lies panic stricken in the early hours
with nothing it can say
it wakes up suddenly on the monitor
urgent and absolute, wanting to sing
the bright music of our daughter
          (this line is written in her laughter)

THE THING IS

The thing is this: you hold them to the light
and laugh, you bring them to me
one in each fist like the edges of a cross
as you wobble over then collapse
you walk the coronation crayon walk
a concentration within a concentration
miraculous: you're pure crayon, nothing but crayon now.

Somewhere over there is paper, somewhere
a line waits for a line like a bus that won't come
but the thing is this: you throw them in the air
you examine them one by one, you put them in the box
and take them out again, the joy of it lifts you to your feet
where you sway with possibility, conducting your colours
and the thing is this, the thing is always this.

RICHES

More than the usual chaos:
the raisin box, the onions,
the potatoes, the small cup,
the brick, the drum,

each solemn offering
searched out and handed over
with such ceremony
I can hardly bear to clear my desk.

More than the usual chaos
let such
unlooked for riches
accompany me always.

I WATCH YOU SLEEP

I watch you sleep, adrift in the giant bed
the door open behind you
the blind trembling in the breeze, world
reaching in, touching your small head

The world sits in your lungs and burns you
is a tangle of wires in an urgent room
the world is here and you've caught
more of it than you should

so do you love it. So let it gather
all around you, flow through you
and wash you back
to this narrow space, the nurses harried

cries down the long corridor
we live within a wafer of each other
and have no special claim
but the door shifts behind your head

the traffic deepens. I lift the blind
and the hills come in, the sudden
glitter of the Cash Bingo hall
as the light touches it, all

the motor factors, hardware stores
and sombre houses of Crumlin
gather round you where you lie
quietly in evening sun.

LE REGRET DE LA TERRE

Jules Supervielle, 1884-1960

One day we'll look back on it, the time of the sun
when light fell on the smallest twig
on the old woman the astonished girl
when it washed with colour everything it touched
followed the galloping horse and eased when he did

that unforgettable time on earth
when if we dropped something it made a noise
and like connoisseurs we took in the world
our ears caught every nuance of air
and we knew our friends by their footsteps

time we walked out to gather flowers or stones
that time we could never catch hold of a cloud

and it's all our hands can master now.

A WEIGHT

Here's a weight: your five thirty
small hands on my face,
your giant grin — hilarious
the sleep of fathers, their faces —
and the dog collapsed on my legs
unmovable. The task is
to keep still and let all of us
drift farther through the dark,
to persuade you from your laughter
to the weight of dream
where you lie lodged between us;
to go nowhere now but stay
with this stalled journey,
hand-held, heart-slowed.
Time enough for light
and lightness, for shifting
unencumbered through the air,
now let the burden hold, and us lie
bone to bone, pressed
to sleep, printed on it, spilled
unchanging type, the day
uncurling fingers from the blind.

FIRST

First door, first handle, first stair
first zip, first sleep, first chair

and now these eyes that must be yours
staring back at you as you brush your hair

first bird, first cat, first car
when I come home I clear your things

I try to hold on as long as I can
and compose the day from your surprise.

HERE YOU ARE

The hedges
already differently configured
the sunlight different on the rushes

but here you are
the two of you
walking up the road

the dog on his extendable lead
extending himself out of view
here are

your badly recorded voices singing
and my own shadow
looming like a net

No reason, maybe,
to choose this one
unhalted moment

no reason
to seek its ceremony
or pull the dog back into view

nothing here
disposed for applause
yet here you are

the two of you
walking the stony road in April
here you are

disposed in light
and the company of trees
and here am I, applauding.

SLIPPING INTO IT

The beautiful, impossible
busyness of it: the darting,
flitting quickness, the panicked
raids and returns, relentless,
rifling the grasses and back
to the gap under the gutter
above the bedroom window

where I place you now
on the deep sill to watch.
'Blue tits,' I say, pointing.
'Blue tits!' you agree, slipping
into it, as if you'd always
known, and this
furious hover above your head

had always been there
waiting to flower. Nothing,
and everything, surprises you
though this, for years,
will pass you by: the desperation
of the labour, how few survive,
how little of what we see

is known to us. But now
the wings beat outside the window,
the sunlit grasses loom
like ships in harbour, and wherever
you look the light arrives,
and the hatches open
on endless, urgent cargoes.

SONG

Even asleep, you're everywhere.
You fall through the house,
right down to the small room
where I sit staring at the screen.
Your head rests on a blinking cursor,
there's a menu for your toes,

you've somehow
drifted into the CD drive
and come out as Janáček,
the overgrown path, the barn owl
lifting its wings. You lurk behind my eyes
and broadcast from my bones

but even miles away, you're on my tongue,
you're banging down the door.
Sometimes I wake in dread
that you might have lifted off
like some bright machine
or vanished music, the owl lurking

in the dangerous dark outside.
What if I couldn't hear you?
As if there were anywhere now
out of reach, as if,
however late it was, or far
I wouldn't hear you breathing

like a wing-beat in the blood,
a song passed from bone to bone . . .

OCTOBER

How she sings   and how everything is in it
how everything is singable   here in October
she sits in the branches of the tree
and a cool sun glitters in the copper

A cool light falls on the floor, glitter
of October   and again she's singing, a soft rope thrown
across the boards, making a song to take us
out to the morning

Glitter of swans on the cold canal, in gold
October quiet in the hard glass of their names
hardly moving   and ourselves hardly moving
the wheels of the bicycle turning but staying

endlessly here in the glitter of this, endlessly stalled.

LIGHTHOUSE

From the history of small journeys
the surf

whirled from the rocks
and raking the road before us

the car park between sea and sea
the mass

of the thick-striped stone
and the houses gathered round it

a whole
village of light

The tea-shop is closing, huge shadows fall
across the finger of land

against which like a fierce argument
the buildings hold their ground

against which everything here
keeps printing and reprinting

the sea hard under heavy sky, such
clarity in flung spray and rocks

the dark could well give up the ghost
and leave us planted on the tarmac

sharp as blades in the edgy dusk
unshiftable as lighthouse stone.

A SHADOW

Along here a birch walk
on the right a grove of alders
avenues of oak and beech
it is a city of trees
where we progress
as from neighbourhood
to neighbourhood
hawthorn to hazel
willow to rowan
here are our childhood streets
the sun streaking
the lower branches: here are
alphabets, adventures
a legend carved in bark
here is our own child
in a family of pines
here is the forest receding
clarifying and receding again
the day floating towards us
then veering off
or straying in its own space
like a rumoured planet
a willow-flicker
bending a shadow
in the watcher's eye
as it circles its sun.

ADVENTURING

How they possess us,
the bullish islands square against the horizon,

the rocks stark in the videotheque,
these

riffs of information
where unanswered questions

strew the paths . . . Mists
of an anorak summer,

fuchsia and scones, our elbows resting
on the squared oilcloth;

we sit in the car and interpret the rain,
we patrol our country

of hoods and maps, of meagre knowledge
flitting in the hedgerows.

Dried crab on the palm, this snail
adventuring on the grass path,

that pure print, as if what we wanted
was to enter so absolutely

we can never be unpeeled
and whatever returns

that must still be us
drifting across the water,

foostering in the branches
or making ready in a cloud,

the three of us
with our endless stuff

setting off again
on the long road to a small place.

AT THE INTERSECTION

Gulls wheel beneath the cranes, spilling sea.
A pigeon flounders, foosters concentratedly
and the 16 comes sharp around the corner.
Playlist after playlist, a random shuffle.

Everything we know will disappear with us.
Step back. Stop, then listen. Then look again and cross
to where butcher, baker, barber is fiddling with the shutter,
closing for the day whatever's still here.

*

We're still here, look: the ruins of the city have risen to meet us.
Raymond Street: you sit in your buggy and flourish the name
    like treasure.
I am wheeling you through masonry, clay, endless riddles of
    detail.
Two grave lollipop men, two free newspapers as we wait for
    the light
where the *Herald AM* intersects with the *Metro*.

*

Pulled over your jeans the reversible princess dress
a dance in pink, a song in blue, then
it's time for the golden slippers, the magic carpet, the log boat
a crocodile is aiming for. Time to be here, and here, and here
just as you are, and perfectly at home in the scatter.

*

You run down the ramp
to stretch for the bell
and a happiness stitched with fear
wafts you in to scope the day.

You hang the journey
on the hook with your name,
allow me one last look,
then turn away.

I go home to coffee, work,
as the dog hangs his hat
on pigeons, cats
and radio voices walk

their streets of chat.
The coffee splutters in its chamber
and dribbles onto the hob
its daily stain. I drain it

in a single draught
and drift to my room,
riding my current
of terrified content . . .

In the Beginning

First comes the idea, someone's dream
of a winding street, of streetlamps.
Then sticks, wattle, ships flaring in the sunset,
serious heads on the coinage. Flagons
of small beer, gin shops, a tax on windows, doors.
Light dapples the civic water, a gallows
ghosts the green. Somehow the cathedral
makes it, somehow the wolf tax is revoked.
The centuries relax, flare up, relax.
The pubs are heaving,
stags and hens, bright buses bear
the sleepless to the suburbs, the conspirators
go over the details of the plan again.
It looks good. Silken Thomas, Isolde's eyelids.
Where is the other side of the street?
Any minute now the bubble-wrapped
department stores, electoral wards, silent armies
of statues. Oh protect us. Someone is singing
'The Foggy Dew', someone is looking out to sea.
No, it must always have been there,
eternal as water, endless as air, the mudflats
singing, the rivers on fire, the districts
ringing out their numbers and their names.

Conversation

I put down the phone
and the years go by.
Twenty years later your voice
is unchanged, as if
as we paused to catch our breath
or press the receiver closer
our bodies lurched from us
and half our lives
fell through the conversation

or we go back and forth
and now as you speak again
I'm sitting on the floor
in an empty office in Merrion Square
clutching an antique phone.
Daily I abandon the typewriter
and the continuous paper
and leave the world on the table

to sneak a call through the crackle
as if we stood on ships in wind
and swayed: our two cities swaying
with small news. My copy's due
my roll of continuous paper
has rolled to the other side of the room
and now, much later, years later
now that the paper's gone
and the line shut down

somehow the conversation continues
somehow we lie in swaying water
and never alter, somehow the line holds
and the years stretch, snap back
and we fall out, come to, send

our signals out, always
finished, unfinished, always
plugged in to a ghostly exchange.

Café Song

There we are
by a pour of willows
in the slender
barge proceeding
from lock to lock
with such leisure
a mile is weeks, months
already they've
forgotten us, and sunk
in narrow spaces
we glide, keep
our eyes on water
and water's edges:
my captain's hat
your trusty
something, the lore
wobbly
for lack of study
a long narrow
house on water
all we wanted
or could imagine:
bed, board and appetite
adrift in the city
nothing to do
but manoeuvre
the racks and gates,
the machinery of slowness
such
stately ascents, delicate
fallings
and through the trees
a sand-bricked terrace
brilliant doors
these journeys

into yellow, into forests
of windows, and the dark
slow ache
of our bodies
in the stalled drift
of the voyage
from a café
hung with canvas
like a huge promise . . .

Lost Cities

They shift under the sands, their ashy streets
and arguable names, lost cities
the silk roads, the quick routes, the palaver
have drifted from —

from one to the other I have gone
dragging my secret bones, my silky tongue.
How lost is lost? Crowds on the temple steps,
the sniff of radar, the dead debriefed again —

Dieter Hofmann, lost father, husband, lover,
your face comes up on the graveyard site,
death is a livingroom in lamplight, whiskey
on a coffee table, you smile at us

from your lonely planet. These cities
beneath our fingers, these swirling stars: the loss
is all ours. We carve our names into the cliff face
and remember ourselves.

The Entry

We did our best we cut the grass we moved the drunks
we listened to you
we planted flowerbeds put up signs
Welcome
300 yew trees
we painted the railings we renovated the chip shop
we put a footpath from the slipway to the ice house
we read the report we painted lobbied objected
we met the developer we read the contract
we buried the wires we landscaped the park
we placed new lights on the street
                the salt wind destroys the flowers
the footpath is broken
from the barracks to the school
the lamps go on and go off again
five times around the holy well
anticlockwise you go
land of the yews and dangerous corners
we took down the railings we met the owner
he refused we pointed out we approached the senator
                the lakes in the back country glitter
next year we will tackle the other side
we cut down the cypresses
                the salt wind destroys the shrubs
we did our best we shifted the lumber
we undid the damage we erected an information panel
we unwrapped the clouds we loosened the weirs
you are here
we returned the salmon we put up stone walls
we built a footpath to the well
and in the distance the mountains
the longest the most beautiful
you are here
beside the handball alley
the salt wind we sang

where the winter scattered its brochures
that gravel is not ours we reported it before
we stayed up late we attached
the chip shop the church the abandoned cottage
we drank everything they had
we spoke to the moon lounging above the weir
we erected the sign we preserved the ruin
we asked the populace to refrain
from diving off the sluice gates
all of us went out in search of litter
through the glittering back country
you are here
you have been standing forever
where the slipway meets the ocean
where the postcards wait in the heritage centre
where every night we would gather
to listen to the sea neglect the forms
the number the details the plans
where the moon hangs its trophies
in the swaying back country.

The Sleep Doctors

You rock yourself to sleep
and then rock sleep,
exciting the polygraphs, bringing
the sleep doctors to the window.

You have always done this,
rocking and dreaming,
startling lovers from your bed,
sleeping yourself alone,

sleeping the deep pure sleep
of yourself, which now they watch,
adding it to the others to show
the wakefulness of sleep.

Whose is the body the child rocks in?
Who are the children,
their foreheads stitched with effort,
returning each night to doctor sleep,

to test for fever, measles, flu;
to smile, confer, prescribe
as cure themselves
gravely rocking, falling asleep in your bones?

Carmina

Worse than ever, shitholes everywhere.
Dig deeper, Catullus, cart your bones
where no one will follow.

*

Even here it continues, fuckers
queuing the length of the alley
to give it to her where she lies
sprawled at leisure, whom I loved
as no one will be loved again.
Even here, waiting his turn,
the ever-smiling Ignatius
with his lovely curls and teeth
brushed with Spanish piss.

*

At every turn a poet reciting
and reciting and reciting and . . .

*

No matter how often I wake
to the shreds of reputation
and go shuffling through halls
lit by scandal, or if I live
a thousand times to come upon her
doling filth on every corner
may I be struck down again and again
if I fail to cry out her name
and perish forever if I do not love her.

*

An energy, somewhere, brings it on,
flash of anger, a passion
islanded in its own rawness
and then I ride my wave
and clamber up the shore again
then the voice is assembled
a current of unease
crackling across the centuries
the door closes for the last time
the door bursts open
the language leaps from its skin again.

*

Tardised
from quay wall to quay wall
the horse trams lumber across the river
car radios
repeat the traffic warning
the place
is alive with haste
and they are all here
again
the earth rinsed from them
wide awake, deodorized
juiced and espressoed
someone's serviceable prick
even now entering her
she moans harshly in the morning
in his tree-lined street
in a southern suburb
plump Ignatius
concludes his toilet with a smile
from dozens of cradles
to as many graves he's carried

his unkillable
idiot's grin
tell him your best friend died
your mother drowned in the river
tell him his wife was seen
out of her brain in the Morrison
the district justice
unhosed around her
and the teeth will blind you with their
impossible glitter.
Come all you chubby Etruscans
you hairy Sabines and ponderous Umbrians
come all you Latvians and Kerrymen
though you wash your teeth in clean water
I couldn't watch you smile forever
still less do I desire the piss-shined grin
of the Celtiberian
whitening the skies of Dublin.

                         *

Go, go, go
everyone
is waiting

they need
one more little book
on its hopeful journey.

Find a spot
on the top shelf
beside the three volumes

of the *History of the Known World*
when you're taken down
maybe you'll have learned something

and maybe the world too
might reach for you
and shift tinily

in its sleep.

*

Let the whispering biddies
lurk in their corner
why should we care?
Let the suns go down and rise again
the dark hand wait
as we touch
in spilled light, and stay
so uncountably here
we lose one another
and no reckoning blight us.

*

Enough stupidity
what's lost is lost.
Once the sun
lightened your days
and you went
where she led you
she'll never be loved
like that again.
How the gods hurried
to hunger us, how

we feasted then
how light your days.
No more of that
panting madness
bring on
the stoic mottoes now.
Be firm, persist,
endure, I
will not bend.
But later, my love
when you've slipped
from the guest list
when no one
remembers your name
who will call for you
whose tongue release you
whose lips will you bite
who will love you then?
Enough stupidity.
Be firm, persist,
endure.

*

Best of all, my friends
now that you've returned
to your beloved family
now your brothers have embraced you
now the calf is sizzling
and your mother's eyes are shining
tell me everything you did
I want to hear your serious voice
explaining the history and geography
the population distribution
the crop yields, the way

you do, drawing your neck
meanwhile closer and closer
until I can kiss
your mouth and eyes again.
Of all men
who is gladder hearted
who more blessed than I?

*

My two good friends
whose lives are linked with mine

who pack a bag and come with me
no matter where I wander

the sad conference in the sticks
the rocky business trip

the boats that time forgot
but the alligators remembered

purgatories of goulash and hard beds
the smarmy satraps in their lairs

who have climbed
and sweated and fallen

and almost died
as we crossed the mountains

who bore desert heat and bitter cold
and would even endure the English

tell her this
tell her I wish her well

may she thrive in the arms
of her three hundred lovers

long life to them
as they pant with exhaustion

each thinking himself
held, beloved

tell her not to look for me
tell her the great love we had

is buried in the wolf lands
in the pit of Asia

tell her it lies in the eastern ocean
in the frozen Arctic wastes

or lies like the flower at the meadow's edge
after the plough has passed.

*

Come to my house tonight
but come prepared
for raw eggs and butter
a little milk, some ancient cheddar.
Even the chairs have gone
the table startled through the door
by four Lithuanian bears.
Why should I grieve? By now
it's already learnt the language

and snorts under quarts of beer.
My jackets fail to remember me
the red chest, the blue lamps
my winter coat. Come
sooner rather than later
while the light hesitates
and the air consults its gods
bring the sweet
Lebanese dancer, her body
all ochred, bring wine and *mezze.*
I'll repay you
with my legendary gaiety
we'll so furnish the night
with dancing and laughter
it will take them another year
to evict the debris from this flat.

*

My dear friend
what exactly were you thinking of?
If I didn't love you more than my own eyes
I'd hate you as we all hate the bastard Vatinius
for this unwelcome gift. Do you really hate me so much
that you reward me with this gaggle of poets?
May the gods infest whoever gave them to you.
They flap and squawk and foul the vestibule.
How can I rest while they're in the house?
Here they go, out with the leftovers, they can
podcast to the rats if they can manage it, ah rats
quick, run for cover before they addle your wits.

*

Who will read these
baroque stupidities
and not flinch from my touch.

*

What
I wouldn't do to you . . .
For you, maybe,
everything written
is the life lived
every image
echoes in the kitchen
every piss pot
sings its song.
The mop and bucket
the milk carton, the bin-liner
and toilet roll are queuing up
to have their say
and if someone touches someone
in a poem of mine
you think my prick
is writing its diaries again
you think I sit
dry-mouthed in the attic
fondling the past
when I could instead
be sprawled with arseholes
in the paradise of literalists
fact-checking the classics.
Whatever house you think
these lines build
if I were you I'd wait a little
before paying the deposit.

*

It's not the winds that blast
your country retreat
but the squalls of an endless mortgage.
How long can it last?
Myhome.ie, thousands of houses
decades of unrest.

*

Days of wine and sestinas
of watching you
take a line and run with it
then bat it back to me across the table.
More often than not
I missed, or lobbed a weak return
for you to smash and win the game.
Back home in the small hours
so taken with it, so fired
by your easy brilliance I couldn't eat
or sleep but thrashed and jittered
like a boy in a poem
and longed for dawn when I could
break down your door again
raining lines as you rubbed your eyes
and grinned. Last night
I lay in a heap on the couch
and somehow wrote these lines
so you can picture my distress.
Don't laugh too hard, don't bin
these prayers, my clever clogs, Nemesis
remember, is an acquaintance of mine
cross her and your greatest poems
will sing you to sleep and vanish forever . . .

*

Farewell Bithynian plains
tonight we sleep in the din of The Tenters
where drinkers slouch from the converted school
and the off-licence opens late
here troubles melt and the mind
lays down its burdens
here the tickets are lost
and the mountains tumble
here's an end to fields and the rippling of lakes
here by the mosque, the boxing stadium,
begins the dog's delirium.
Freed from himself he buries his nose
in the stink of the city.
Home! he snorts, and so do I.

*

And if you're going to ask me
ask me now I'm on my bed
lunched, loosened

unzipped
little Ipsitilla, unhinged
but rock solid and ever ready.

*

We girls and virgin boys
are Diana's, come

sing Diana now, child
of Latona, child of Jupiter

born by the Delian olive-tree
that you might always be

our lady of the mountains
and the green woods

our lady of the secret valleys
and the teeming rivers

hallowed be what name
you will, now and ever

keep us safe.

                    *

Another winter closes in.
Zukovsky and Celia at the table again
fulsere quondam candidi tibi soles
'Full, sure once, candid the sunny days glowed, solace . . .'

Ah!

                    *

Worse every day.
Worse every hour.
What exactly
would you have me say?
Would it have been
such a hardship to visit?
Have postmen vanished?
Has paper been swept from the world?
You who know me well
who understand my passion

send a few words of comfort
a postcard from Spar
a stanza or two
from the *Penguin Book of Despair*
the girl handing out papers on the corner
with her smile and her long hair.

*

Her face pouts from the festival poster:
interviewed and fêted
she's back, she's hot, she's
radioed and late lated, her life
spills out, juicy, surely
this heart must break
one part revelation
to three parts self-deception.
I drink my coffee
sweetened by pain
the host
drymouthed with desire
the very dust bristling
with erectile despair
she pours
the slow honey of herself
into the nation's ear.

*

What's this —
Catullus among the hedgerows
lake-lorn and rained on

where thick-bunched clouds
fill the sky, a blue light hard
behind them

and the meadow falls in waves
pheasant scrape, curlew
the white willows flutter

the light idles with the rain
over and back all afternoon
the thing still undecided

my eyes the net
stretched between them, my entire
body robed, gloomed, brightened

so much happening
I can't stay in
so much that happens

is beyond us
whose small wits encompass little
a sudden hand turns the sky up

blink once
and a galaxy is gone
the gods have lived and died.

＊

If any sweetness stirs in earth, Calvus,
if anything in that silence brings
old loves stealing across the grass again
and nudges friends to stroll
hand in hand down the avenues, then surely
Quintilia might turn again
her delicate head towards you
and sorrow at her early death be swayed
by the warming pleasure of your love for her.

*

Questioned, searched, passed on
from barrier to border, crossing
by night and day, through
torn cities, through

the held breath of valleys
through famine, fire and stench
to stand
under a strange sky with the customary offerings

to bend my silence to yours and know
the gentlest breath will never reach you
the fiercest word.

I bring you buried streets
and fallen hills
the dust of your own house
the black cloak of my voice.

Lost brother
here in alien air
I stand in your arms that have left me forever.

*

What now
the song is over?
Make it again
the sweet
disaffected dance of it,
imagine this music made
in the ditches of time,
in pools of streetlight
across the planet

coming to
in the swaying tram
still at it, still here
thicktongued with want
and rubbing your finger
on the misted window to see
the brutal, lovely
persistence of the city.

Acknowledgements and Notes

Thanks are due to the editors of the following publications in which these poems, or versions of them, have appeared: *Agenda, Best of Irish Poetry 2008, Irish Pages, Poetry Europe, Salt Magazine, Southword, The Stinging Fly, The Warwick Review* and *The Watchful Heart — a New Generation of Irish Poets: Poems and Essays.*

The author acknowledges also the assistance of a bursary from An Comhairle Ealaíon/The Arts Council, Ireland, in the completion of this collection.

page 12   Jordi Savall i Bernadet was born in 1941, in Igualada, Catalonia, Spain. A Spanish-Catalan viol player, conductor and composer, he has been one of the major figures in the field of early music since the 1970s, largely responsible for bringing the viol (viola da gamba) back to life on the stage. His repertoire ranges from Mediaeval to Renaissance and Baroque music.